AN
INTERVIEW
WITH
SANTA CLAUS

AN
INTERVIEW
WITH
SANTA CLAUS

BY
MARGARET MEAD
AND
RHODA METRAUX

WALKER AND COMPANY
NEW YORK

Picture Credits:

Nast, Thomas, *Christmas Drawings For The Human Race,* Harper & Bros., 1890. *Front and back covers, pp. 12; 18; 24; 30; 34.*

Nast, Thomas, *Harper's Weekly.* pp. 14, 1884; 36, 1881; 42, 1872, 44, 1874; 48, 1879.

Harper's Weekly. pp. 10, "The Christmas Tree," 1858; 28, Jules Taverner, lithograph, "The Christmas Dream," 1871; 46, Unsigned lithograph, 1869.

The Night Before Christmas, Raphael Tuck & Sons Co., Ltd., *pp. 8; 26.*

Christmas card published by Louis Prang, Boston 1888. *p. 16.*

Seventeenth-century Russian mosaic icon, Middle Eastern Technical University, Ankara. *p. 20.*

Eighteenth-century French print. *p. 22.*

Illustrated Ethiopian Manuscript, probably eighteenth century. *p. 32.*

Santa Arriving in Sidney, Australia (Australia News and Information Bureau). *p. 38.*

Nineteenth-century greeting card from the collection of E. Willis Jones. *p. 40.*

FRONTISPIECE BY R. METRAUX

Copyright © 1978 by Margaret Mead and Rhoda Metraux

First published in *Redbook Magazine,* December, 1977.

First published in the United States of America in 1978 in book form by the Walker Publishing Company, Inc.

Published simultaneously in Canada by Beaverbooks, Limited, Pickering, Ontario.

ISBN: 0-8027-0620-7

Library of Congress Catalog Card Number: 78-62994

Printed in the United States of America

10 9 8 7 6 5 4 3 2 1

DESIGNED BY JUDITH WORACEK

to Kate

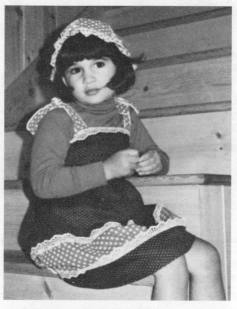

PREFACE

Some 20 or 30 years ago—and for a long time before that—one could not get through the Christmas season without reading, or reading about, a sentimental bit of writing known as "Yes, Virginia, There Is a Santa Claus." It was an editorial written in 1897 by Francis Pharcellus Church and published by him in the New York Sun in the form of an open letter to a young girl named Virginia O'Hanlon. The letter was so convincing that people used to say it made even grown-up grumps into firm believers in Santa Claus. I don't know if it did or didn't, but I can tell you it did move a lot of us to think twice about disbelief in the season's patron saint.

The world has grown a lot warier of myths, legends and fairy tales since Virginia was a child, and while Santa Claus definitely is still around, belief in him either as a reality or a possibility has dwindled. Or if it hasn't, it surely has been swallowed up in the excess of hullabaloo and hoopla that surrounds the season these days. Or so it seems — until along comes someone to set Santa up again and welcome him back.

In December, 1977, in *Redbook Magazine,* Margaret Mead and Rhoda Metraux, Contributing Editors to the magazine, wrote what we believe will become the new classic Christmas story. In it they not only welcomed Santa Claus to the holiday season, they sat down and talked with him (or her!). Is there a Santa Claus? Read this lovely little book and decide for yourself.

SEY CHASSLER
EDITOR-IN-CHIEF
Redbook Magazine

The Night Before Christmas

FATHER TUCK'S NURSERY FRIENDS SERIES

"FOR THREE MONTHS HER FAVORITE BEDTIME READING HAS BEGUN ''TWAS THE NIGHT BEFORE CHRISTMAS . . .'"

Kate has discovered Santa Claus. For three months her favorite bedtime reading has begun, " 'Twas the night before Christmas, when all through the house . . ." Every visitor is subjected to her eager questioning: "Do you know Santa Claus? Where does he live? Does he bring you presents too? Is he very old? How does he come to your house?"

Kate is three-going-on-four, just the age when a small girl's curiosity and imagination know no bounds and everything she learns leads to more questions. Later she probably won't remember asking or who tried to answer her endless questions, but the gist of what she found out will be there in her memory bank forever.

"...GIVING AND RECEIVING PRESENTS."

Of course, this is the time of year when children everywhere in America are wondering about Santa Claus, and parents and grandparents everywhere are hard pressed to find answers that are both true in some way and faithful to their feelings about children and Christmas and giving and receiving presents.

For some questions there are fairly simple answers: Who are the men, wearing Santa Claus suits and ringing their bells, on the many street corners? Well, they're pretend Santa Clauses; they're asking us to help make Christmas a little merrier for people who don't have homes like ours.

"...THE SANTA CLAUS."

And what about the jolly Santa Claus, sitting on a kind of throne in the department store, who invites you to come and tell him your wishes? No, he's not *the* Santa Claus either. He's one of Santa Claus's helpers, waiting for you to talk to him.

But the other questions, the harder ones that Kate and her nursery-school friends are asking—how do we answer them? What children want, really, is a biography of Santa Claus. And thinking about him, we found we were calling him *The* Santa Claus the way Scottish clans call their senior member The Macgregor or The MacDonald.

"WHAT IF WE COULD RING HIM ON THE TELEPHONE . . ."

What if we could ring him on the telephone and ask for an interview? If we could dial Information (where?) and ask for Santa's home number—Or would it be his office? How would it go? Let's see. . . .

"CHILDREN ARE ASKING MANY QUESTIONS . . ."

MARGARET MEAD AND RHODA METRAUX: Is this *The* Santa Claus?

SANTA CLAUS: I suppose you might say so, yes.

M & R: Are you really alive?

SANTA: I certainly am—and very busy these days, too.

M & R: But do you have a few minutes for an interview? Children are asking so many questions, and we don't know the answers.

SANTA: Go ahead. I'll do my best.

"HOW CAN YOU BE IN SO MANY PLACES AT ONCE?"

M & R: First, are you one person or many? How can you be in so many places at once?

SANTA: Of course *I'm* one person. But I belong to a very big clan and a very old one—a clan of givers. As far as I know, our history goes back at least two thousand years, and maybe much longer, but when you get back that far, it's all hearsay and tales that are almost like fairy tales.

". . . A VERY FAMOUS BISHOP
IN THE EARLY CHRISTIAN CHURCH . . ."

M & R: Who was your first ancestor you know about for sure? Was he a jolly man just like you?

SANTA: Not at all. He was a very different kind of man—a very famous bishop in the early Christian church in Asia Minor in the fourth century. A very solemn man. Pictures always show him dressed in cloth of gold and looking very stern. But he loved children and young people. Once he secretly gave a bag of gold coins to each of three poor sisters so they would have a dowry and could find husbands.

"ONCE HE BROUGHT BACK TO LIFE THREE LITTLE BOYS . . ."

He performed lots of miracles, too. Once he brought back to life three little boys who'd been chopped up and salted in barrels by a wicked innkeeper. And he calmed a storm and saved a ship at sea. He even appeared in a dream to the great Emperor Constantine to tell him that three of his officials had been falsely accused, and the Emperor had them released from prison. He became a saint, you know—St. Nicholas, they called him—and he was the friend of sailors and travelers and merchants, but especially the friend of children.

"But how did he leave Asia Minor and come to Europe?"

M & R: But how did he leave Asia Minor and come to Europe?

SANTA: Well, there are two different stories about that. If you go to Bari, in Italy, they will tell you that when the Turks were laying waste to his home city of Myra in 1084, some merchants brought St. Nicholas' bones to Bari and built him a wonderful shrine to which pilgrims came—still come—from far and wide. But if you go to Venice, they'll tell you *their* merchants rescued his bones in 1100 and built him the great Church of St. Nicholas, on the Lido. But who can say which it was? And does it matter? He was a favorite saint for a long, long time. In England before the Reformation there were three hundred and seventy-six churches in his name and hundreds more in Belgium and Holland, France and Italy, and especially in Russia, and in Greece and other places too. Everybody loved that saint, our ancestor, and "Santa Claus" is a version of that ancestor's name.

"... AND THE CHILDREN HUNG UP STOCKINGS ..."

M & R: But what in the world did St. Nicholas have to do with Christmas and giving presents?

SANTA: You see, his birthday was in December—the sixth of December, by our calendar today—and people celebrated his birthday with a feast. The night before, children in lots of places put out little bundles of hay for the white horse or the donkey he rode—of course, it was really one of his descendants, one of our clan, who came. And the children put out a shoe or hung up a stocking and the members of my clan were kept busy, I can tell you, filling them up with fruit and candy and little cakes—celebrating by *giving* presents instead of receiving them. But we had a lot of trouble too.

"... SCARY CREATURES ..."

M & R: How was that?

SANTA: Well, they say that in some places, parents didn't think children should be given presents just for nothing. They wanted good children to be rewarded and bad children to be punished. So some of our clan had to pretend to be scary creatures that came along with old St. Nick. The most famous, I guess, was Knecht Ruprecht, a frightening being who carried a switch. Another one was called Klaubach, a kind of shaggy monster with horns and fiery eyes and a long red tongue and chains that clattered! There were lots of others, equally fearsome, but I've always thought all this was done to impress the grownups. I've never heard that children were actually punished or didn't get their presents. And nowadays we've given all that up. All our clan want to be the children's *friend*.

"... WE'RE ALL GIFT-GIVERS TO CHILDREN."

M & R: Are all your clan descended from St. Nicholas?

SANTA: Some of them, I'm not sure how we're related. What holds us together is that we're all gift-givers to children. Some of the gift-givers are girls and women, you know. There's St. Lucia, for one, whose feast day is December thirteenth. In Sweden the prettiest girl in the house used to play St. Lucia. Wearing a white dress and a crown with nine lighted candles, she used to wake the household before dawn. In some parts of Austria, St. Lucia brought presents for the girls and St. Nicholas brought them for the boys.

M & R: It seems to us we remember something about an old woman, too.

SANTA: That must be Babushka, who used to bring presents—well, she still does—to children in Russia. She's the ancestor I've always felt most sorry for.

M & R: Sorry for? Why is that?

SANTA: Well, they tell different stories, but it always comes to the same thing. Some people remember that Babushka was spinning when the Magi—the Three Wise Men—stopped at her door and invited her to go with them to visit the newborn King. But she said she had to finish her spinning, and of course, the Magi couldn't wait. And so ever after she has wandered around looking for the Baby.

"... FLEEING TO EGYPT ..."

Other people say that she turned away the Holy Family while they were fleeing to Egypt and when she realized what she had done she ran after them—too late. Whatever the truth, she goes out every year at Christmas and gives presents on His birthday to all children in His name. And in Italy we have another ancestor, Befana, another old woman, who brings children presents on Twelfthnight, which is, you know, January sixth, the day of the Magi.

M & R: Were the Magi also your ancestors?

SANTA: No, I don't think so. But in a way it was from them that we got the idea of giving gifts to children, just as they brought gold and myrrh and frankincense to the newborn Baby in Bethlehem. Maybe they're honorary ancestors. And in some places we helped out.

" . . . WE'VE HAD TO GO EVERYWHERE . . ."

In Provence long ago, children used to go out into the country on Twelfth-night to meet the Kings, taking them presents of food for themselves and their pages and their horses. And the Kings gave the children presents in return. And *somebody* had to play the role of the Kings! In fact, we've had to go everywhere and change with times and places. So we have lots of names and different faces.

"... WE DEVELOPED A WHOLE NEW LIFE STYLE ..."

M & R: I can see that. But, Santa Claus, let's come back to you.

SANTA: Oh, that's an exciting saga in itself. You know my immediate ancestors came to America with Dutch and German families. We were immigrants. And like all the other immigrants, we developed a whole new life style as we became Americans. For instance, most of us took a new name, Santa Claus—though some people still talk about me as "old St. Nick." And most of us concentrate on Christmas nowadays, instead of scattering our efforts, so all the children can enjoy getting presents at once.

" . . . AND IN SOME PLACES IN SPEEDBOATS."

M & R: And by now you're an Old American!

SANTA: And a modern one too. Those first pictures of us, about a hundred years ago, seem pretty old-fashioned now. With those reindeer and all that.

M & R: What do you mean? Don't you still have your reindeer?

SANTA: Oh, yes, but you know, nowadays we have to go so far. At first we just went around different parts of America. But now children everywhere in the world expect Santa Claus to arrive with presents, all at practically the same time. We can't disappoint children just because they happen to live on the other side of the world. So I—or, rather, we—have to travel in helicopters and airplanes, even sometimes in snowmobiles and in some places in speedboats.

"... I'M VERY FOND OF THE REINDEER MYSELF."

M & R: Then why do you keep the reindeer at all?

SANTA: Oh, the children would be too sad if I gave them up, and I'm very fond of the reindeer myself. Besides, there's a legend about a man—or maybe he was a god—who is said to have been one of our earliest ancestors. Thor, his name was, and people say that in the Far North, in midwinter, he used to come rushing down on the wind, bringing snow and ice and driving a team of reindeer. I wouldn't want to forget that, even if maybe it's only a legend. And I love to hear the reindeer bells. Listen! Can't you hear them too?

"OF COURSE IT HAD BEEN A DREAM."

We listened and we did hear them. Faint at first and then very loud, and woke to hear the telephone ringing. Of course, it had been a dream.

A dream, yes. But it makes a kind of sense, doesn't it? Why shouldn't there be a whole clan of gift-giving figures? Don't they all, in some way, convey a special message to children? St. Nicholas and St. Lucia and other favorite saints, friends of children, the grandmother figures of Babushka and Befana and others of their kind, Santa Claus in all his different versions, each with a special name, and sometimes the Three Kings and even the old Norse god Thor, coming down into the known world from the unknown North with his reindeer.

"... IN THE MIDST OF WINTER ..."

All of them have appeared on some day close to the shortest day of the year, when the very sharpness of a cold, barren winter gives promise of spring, so that long ago, in the midst of winter, human hearts rejoiced and were moved to generosity and gaiety, especially for children.

"... GIVING AS WELL AS RECEIVING ..."